Fishing for Family

Fishing for Family

Poems by

Anthony DiMatteo

© 2019 Anthony DiMatteo. All rights reserved.
This material may not be reproduced in any form, published,
reprinted, recorded, performed, broadcast,
rewritten or redistributed without
the explicit permission of Anthony DiMatteo.
All such actions are strictly prohibited by law.

Cover art: Christina Bothwell, "Mermaid"
Cover design: Shay Culligan

ISBN: 978-1-950462-17-9

Kelsay Books Inc.

kelsaybooks.com

502 S 1040 E, A119
American Fork, Utah 84003

For My Brother

Acknowledgments

I thank the National Park Service for awarding an artist-residency at Fire Island, N.Y. My thanks also go to the editors of these publications where versions of these poems first appeared:

Weatherings—An Anthology: "Assistive Living"

One: "Citizens of the Universe"

American Society—What Poets See: "County Fair, Memorial Day"

Pirene's Fountain: "Father Time"

Clade Song: "Fishing for Family"

UCity Review: "Little Fish," Canyon Call," "The One Truth," "Snapshot under Water"

Levure Littéraire: "Mimicry," "Works in Progress"

The Ekphrastic Review: "River of Light," "Dark Matter"

Suffolk County Poetry Review: "Rummaging in New Hampshire"

Naugatuck River Review: "Sacrifice"

Poets East—An Anthology of Long Island Poets: "The Breach (Fire Island National Wilderness)"

The Lake—Contemporary Poetry Webzine: "The Pelt"

Boomer Lit Mag: "The Stream (Laurel Prong, Virginia)"

Grey Sparrow Journal: "To Joseph Roulin, Postman, Facing Van Gogh"

Innisfree Poetry Journal: "When Nothing's Left"

Contents

Proem (Little Fish)

I Childhood

Acculturation	17
Mother Tongue	18
My Mother's Penis	20
Life Lesson	24
Snapshot Under Water	25

II Adolescence

County Fair, Memorial Day	29
Citizens of the Universe	31
Sacrifice	32
Hurt in Love (Don't Ask)	33

III Adulthood

Fishing for Family	37
The Stream (Laurel Prong, Virginia)	39
The One Truth (to Kathleen)	40
The Pelt	42
When Nothing's Left	43

Rummaging in New Hampshire	44
Canyon Call	45
Mimicry	47
Painting the Light	49
The Breach (Fire Island National Wilderness)	51
The Slant Light (for Michael)	52
Inside the Teaching Machine	53

IV Senescence

Works in Progress	57
The Portent	60
The Grandfathers	61
Red Cup, Yellow Leaves	62
Assistive Living	63

Epilogue (Transport)

Proem (Little Fish)

I went to buy you a goldfish
in a small glass bowl
but the man told me it would grow
to the size of the rainbow koi
swimming in a large tank.
"This is why the fish die
people take back from a fair."

Later, in the rain, a blue
thought drifted by me.
Can a life outgrow its home?
If so, must we shrink the soul
to where we stand? Hope
pared down to a chink
coming through a door
the way a fish in a globe
has the one view on a shelf?
Should it tip, the fish'll find
all's not made of water
though light stays the same
on both sides of the bowl.

In the end, I didn't buy the fish
but give you this poem instead.
It wiggles out of my hands
to seek you in your world.

I Childhood

Acculturation

Who needs words when a nod of the head
does the trick? Toddler befuddles mom
and doc who says the child lags the norm.
Yet when he cries "e e," she cuts a beeline.
How fast depends on how many e's.
Lighting her up with a wiggle and grin,
he leads her by hand to what brings him glee.
All the world to her, he gives her a spin.

Who needs words when a nod of the head
makes one feel like a god? He'll be told
even God died and his mom foresaw the woe,
paradise lost when we came to know.
But for now the boy's cute as hell and pulls
her strings. All that charm? Good for sales.

Mother Tongue

> "Is there a human voice, a voice that is the voice of man as the chirp is the voice of the cricket or the bray the voice of the donkey?"
> —Giorgio Agamben, *Infancy and History*

A child has a way of voicing other
than a parent's, a different way
of seeing, of feeling. The child's quest
regards what the body loves. That'll grow
into spirit when the child reaches age.

A way of speaking becomes a way of living
amounting to more than words can say.
Love and loss come into being, mountain
top experiences with no mountain in sight.
What can one say to the silence when

she doesn't come, when night has done
its damage and the blizzard taken its toll?
We grow up fast because we have to sprout
and because the music stops when she
does not come. We have to go it alone.

Still we call out, addressing mountains,
imitating the wolf or chanting to the birds.
The echo rings back human to our ears.
We say what we are but are not what we say.
This is why a child laughs at the noises

that become names, calling out mother,
watching her appear, opening our mouth,
our tongue a reed, a magic wand.
We laugh or cry and learn to play the game,
which sounds lure, which ones only rave.

We are told who we are by what we say,
falling into a place other than our own.
Words will harden us in the grind of sense,
our bodies turned a numbered vehicle,
not the wondrous thing we are when born,

to which state the deepest third of us wishes
to return, wrapped in a cloud of wonder,
a fish in an endless sea of light,
but tethered to the one who comes and goes,
she who brings food and song in equal share.

We'll open on our own, windows and doors,
and the bond with our mother—if strong—
leads out to a voyage in radiance
the earth offers in every field and road.
But a wearying world lies in wait.

A way of speaking becomes a way of living
like a waterfall cutting through stone
it has polished there for centuries,
the discards of eroding mountains,
the waters alive and in a hurry.

My Mother's Penis

I Honor

Tripping off to the pool, we crammed
into the station wagon, my sister seated
next to me with her suspiciously large breasts.
I had no idea how big until the horny boys
older than me who lived down the block
made me drink my first beer while they
danced about with a cushion jammed up
their t-shirt imitating my oldest sister.
"She's got Almond Joys," they teased me,
messing my hair as I downed the beer.
When I told my sister, she smiled at first,
then remembered to show her scorn.
"Why didn't you defend me and beat them up?"
My other sister tried to save my honor.
"You know you love that they noticed,"
she told her. I felt queasy from the beer
and the smirch. But then the day ahead
at the pool would make me lurch even more.

II Of Biblical Proportions

I recall the first time I saw him naked.
The seven of us arrived in our swim trunks,
my two older sisters in their polka dot
bikinis to go with the song, bombshells
in their mind like the atoll. It did not matter
to my father and me what we wore, what men
since the time of Abraham have worn
for a swim, those shorts. And I've learned

it shouldn't matter to men though women
have gone from bloomers to g-strings.
After our swim and picnic, my father
and I retired to the men's locker room.
"Make sure you scrub all that chlorine off,
my little fish," my mother said as she
patted me on the rear. That embarrassed me
but nothing like when I turned to see
my father standing there with that lump
between his legs and all that black hair
like a bald eagle in its nest. To tell true,
I did not know what to make of it
although I knew it was partly where I had
come from, if I could believe my friends.
It thus belonged to mother as much as him,
one of my makers, that fat finger of flesh.

III Shame

But all that hair? Where does it come from?
When would it flare up? Do you have to comb
and keep it trim? His had all wild knots
like a brillo pad crunched over a hose.
My father caught me looking and hollered.
"What's your problem? You got one too!
Get dressed." I could barely loop my belt.
I felt my face turn red in confusion
and shame, bed buddies as they are.
From the look on my face, my mother
could tell my world had been spilled.
"Are you OK?" "He's fine," my father said,
nudging me along into the backseat.

IV Mother Nature

On the trip back home, I had the window seat
and could tune-out. Past the bridge
between the Jersey cliffs and New York,
I loved how the river didn't stop
to pay the toll, showing no respect
for the division of states. Boats too
didn't pay, but not in the way fish
and the birds don't. We whirred
by the thick maples that line
Pelham Parkway, where ten years on
a girl would first touch me below.
As we drove up the driveway, I doubted
mine would ever get to be like his.

V Father Time

That night I took a long, closer look.
How could this squirty thing do so much?
I had more to learn then—and still have.
Those little balls aswim in their pink sac
would help bless two wives with a fine child,
girl and boy. Now one's tested for cancer
and might go before it spreads to its twin.
We prove guests of our body bound to its fate.
But what then did I know of love or loss?
My wisdom still makes the briefest chapter.

VI The Wound

Two weeks past the revelation of the pool,
my friend Ben and I were changing after sports
when I accidentally noticed how different
he looked from me below but not in the way
my father did. No, in length and girth
and in baldness, the same as mine
or even my baby brother's, but Ben's
had a flappy hat on it like a mushroom.
"Stop looking," he told me. Later on,
I asked my father about that and he said,
"Oh get off that topic," so I had to ask
my mother and she told me all about it.
I was glad mine had the approved form
though I still was leery about the whole
direction it would take, especially the hair.
That had to itch, no? Of course, it must,
but I had no idea at the time of that
inner burning no scratching can reach.

Life Lesson

When I saw that envy was a snake
that bites you in the back of your head,
coming out of your own mouth, I thought
why would anyone lie? One nun—I forget
her name—would draw sins on the board
in colored chalk, green for the snake,
red rooster for lust, black for the blind
bull of anger, hot pink for the pig.
She left her brightest color for the gold
lute of the devil who was in the guise
of a monkey seated in the middle,
tanned maestro of the vices. How easy
to stay good, I fancied, how stupid,
evil. The beasts around me stood out
in a crowd like a sloth at noonday
or a camel wandering around a mall.
I spotted pride's trance in the lives
of others, spellbound by my own.
The gold lute of self-deceit I'd play
alone, my own monkey in a cage.
The mirror of lust I mistook for real,
my own sun in a world of darkness.
But that false light would black out
each time I'd go and hurt those I love.
The path to what's right has will in the way.
Over time, a child in me would recall
the horror once felt at the human zoo
the Sister had chalked on the board,
the dust of her drawings like the ashes
we become, and the music of the monkey
seldom silent and easy to succumb.

Snapshot Under Water

People love the bay they don't swim in
anymore. These two girls, though,
lay face down in the brown tide.
At the lip of the shore, they are wrapped up
in the warm water and in each other,
not noting the little boat that's pulled up
and the two gray men stepping out.
Their anchor will not hold in the soft sand,
but the gaze of the girls that kept out the world
will summon childhood years hence
when a first friend moves away at last
and that bay beach is all boarded up.

II Adolescence

County Fair, Memorial Day

Girls with ski hats pulled tight, high
heels and shorts, fat dudes
wearing skeletons on t-shirts, rings
in noses, tongues and ears, tattoos
of dragons, baby shoes, dropping bombs,
the face of Jesus turning an arm
into Veronica's veil—and that's just the line
queuing up for the Zipper ride. Come
and see the show. Which one? Across the way,
Alice, a magician's large white rabbit,
pees on a little boy offered up
by his parents. Children and animals
are sure to make us reach. Wolves—
WILD WOLVES the sign insists—
pace back and forth as the smell
of sausage fills the air. Do we smell
like pigs to them while we text
madly waiting for the horror house?
(Nimble hooves work tiny keys.) I look up
into the eyes of the alpha male, "gold brown
the better to see at night," the hawker tells me,
but who needs to see inside a cage?
Now the wolves look lost amidst
a gawking crowd. I recall
the terror that ran up my spine alone
and lost in Maine out in the woods
when in the distance as the sun set
I thought I heard one howl. Out of the wild,
invisible walls close in. We're trained
to walk a fine line at specific times,
this room, then that, as the world assigns
mine and thine and splits us apart,

pacing back and forth. We duck our heads
when a three-gun salute to the troops goes off.
When I played with toy soldiers,
I was always the safe general far away.
Now my fantasy's to join a circus
traveling up and down the east coast
or the big highways out west, living
with a tribe of fellow free ones,
bit of straw in our mouths as we sit
exhausted after hauling out tents.
Someone starts blowing a harp.
Trying to rescue my orphaned dream,
I shuffle through the sweaty crowd
to speak to a woman working a stand.
Lou Ann her nameplate says. She looks
up with tired eyes when I call to her,
then laughs and shakes her head as we chat.
"Boy, got its moments, but the magic's gone.
The work's hard and there's barely time off."
Later I see her walk by through the mass
of us, making her way to the trailer park
new sprung in some parking lot seen
by outsiders only from the Ferris wheel—
potted plants and satellite dishes,
a few residents mulling about smoking
as the night drops down on all of us.

Citizens of the Universe

At seventeen I found out my mother
was adopted. The purity of my blood
proved so much snow in July.
Thought old enough to know the truth,
I looked at her with new eyes. She
was told at seventeen by her mother.
My own shock gave way to hers,
how she must have suffered,
how she must have wondered.
Half-French, half-German, was she
an abandoned product of the great war?
I embraced her the way children do,
not needing to know each other's names.

Sacrifice

Tall buildings with a sun between
out of nowhere appear, and I am walking
into a shop with sawdust on wooden floors
receding into shadow. Casements of glass
gleam with red meats neatly trimmed,
and I know where I am, my father's father's
shop long since torn down. I wait for him
though he died before I was born.
I see the sovereign remains of his work
on brown waxed paper at my knees.
Blood begins to drip down the glass.
Eye-high, atop a metal counter, a lamb
has been slaughtered, its neck sliced,
and where the wound is open
flowers pour into my hands.
Above me, I see a shadow flash
across a white sky, so I awake,
remembering not to end the dream.
I am cut off from it, from him, from the past,
the way sun and earth edge each other apart
for light to glow on all the Easter days.
Dreams and poems butcher us all,
and we them, but they strike without blade.

Hurt in Love (Don't Ask)

You say don't ask yet still I know.
In your face do I see sorrow
which after love may hold a place?
Desire so fleet leaves no trace.
I must grow indifferent to you
should a hard night recall our glow.
By its light, I'll write rondeaux
that teach me how to erase.
You say don't ask.
Was it not yourself you did show?
What I thought deep was only floe?
I may not be hard to replace.
You did not swallow, only taste.
Can there be more of you to know?
You say don't ask.

III Adulthood

Fishing for Family

I wake to find my brother has a pike on the line too big to reel in early one morning. We're at large in the Smokies, a whole day free to roam, high for me, low for him. He stays lakeside. I hike up to Mt. Shuckstack and climb a shaky fire tower. A brown hawk rips by. Two women roll in and pee, too late for me to call down. Then three sweaty dudes show up. One drops into the cool grass right where one woman peed. I laugh so hard Gatorade chuffs out my nose and am discovered sixty feet up. "Guess we weren't alone," she says. I wait till they all leave, saving us from mutual embarrassment. The silence I had been sharing with the hawk floods back.

> Anything can show on the AT. It turns
> strangers soulmates or soulmates strangers.
> Round any bend, flowers, toads, crow or hobo,
> but mostly, the deep peace of the woods.

Hours later I find my brother wearing snakeskins. He had long since set a pike free and gone for a cold swim to an island where he thought he heard a bear. When I tell him I'd seen two women piss, he knows I'm not lying. Why say two when one will do? "Sure gonna pole your pike on that one tonight," he ribs. The way out the next day I hear a bird hiss. Am I near a nest? I look up: nothing. I look down: five-foot rattler, head raised, spitting at my knee. I freeze, then slowly back out the strike zone. I warn my brother trailing behind. He doesn't believe me but then sees with his own eyes. "Holy fuck," he yells. I reply: "Ye, and let dust be its food." He looks for a rock. I ask, "Why?" It was returning to the green silence of the cool glade. We stand amazed.

> Possibilities swirl, stars in a stream.
> Often we flat out don't see or see
> only what we believe we can see.
> Then someone leaves. The light changes.

What if the snake had bit me eight miles out from the car? What if there had been six women and I fell—or was thrown—from the tower? What if my brother got lost or drowned and I found the pike cold on the grill or it had been lost to the bear? Enough happens in the woods even when nothing does. But the backdrop of silence against which we hear a waterfall or our own foot fall is an ocean or night immense with stars.

> The annihilation that is death
> feels closest in the woods.
> We see nothing human there
> to distract us from who we are.

But now, many years later, the feeling is everywhere. My brother was murdered by three thieves who broke into his house and stabbed him with his own kitchen knife as if they had mistaken him for a fish whose life they had the right to take. Since then, my faith more often than not has failed me. I can't see what side of the fence wilderness is on, and I wonder about the kindness of the kin we call mankind.

> Can you not hear in any room
> much less a forest or the sky
> how quiet things are without us?

The Stream (Laurel Prong, Virginia)

Nothing changes much more slowly here
than this stream in the wood that alters
with the seasons. The coming highways
will not eradicate its source just as rutted
it remains from an ice age when
a boulder trailed a finger to carve it
in its bed. Not far from here in a cabin,
a president and prime minister decided
the size of the greatest navies of the world,
but only leaves have sailed on this river's
prong. I have slept on its meandering
banks and heard the chatter of leaves
that have come and gone and wondered
how long stars will remain tangled
in the canopies above. Seldom does it seem
to notice man, erasing walks once set
by a small band of Marines. I admit
I have sought acceptance of my presence
before the quiet shimmer of its waters,
asking for its blessings on those I love—
the secret offices of my religion
in which I hail it as one of my saints.

The One Truth (to Kathleen)

I was in Nevada and the road was
moving under me, or was I on the road
in Montana as mountains fled?

The wind rose and the night stumbled
into the woods. You were on my mind
the way I had been on the road.

I was along my way trackless
before you appeared. I could not pass
beyond your trace—what use

to look to bluffs of Wyoming,
those pinnacles of sand?
Where an open field let yel-

low flowers wander for miles
I found one of your thrilling routes
under stars and no speed limit.

I watched mountains rise up
as if wearing the breath of God
and three rivers converge

in a wild concourse of silver
headstrong for a distant sea.
I beheld the moon ride above

blackened valleys, and it wore
your face, mocking my quest.
In the far sweep of your current,

I turned into a stream seeking
where I ended and you began.
The waters proved to merge.

But the dimmer the woods,
the darker the night, the more
the one truth remains clear:

I will return to you.

The Pelt

There at the back of the closet,
suitcase smug in zippered dust.
You swear it's mine, loaded with a flock
of secrets waiting for daylight
to burst out of the silence of the past.
Burn or bury it? Push it back deeper?

I know it is not mine. We open it
and the extent of your mother's
obsession becomes clear. As if plucked
from your head by her dead fingers,
bagged locks of hair more than thirty years old,
one for every year until you married

your first husband, the one whose arms
she urged you to, longing to leave
your father, you the last child to go,
and when you did, she fled a thousand miles
from him, from all she knew, and now
we ponder her sad dream of your

eternal youth and how she longed
for it not to end as our fingers let go
and the strands fly off in the wind.

When Nothing's Left

Dancers suddenly leave the studio stage
and out comes this guy from the back
stumbling, dressed in a shaggy mat,
wilderness man lost at center floor,
bouncing a bit on his haunches
like he's got hot coals in his pocket.
He places in a circle what looks like stones,
little loaves of bread perhaps, but when
he starts hopping around them,
I bust out laughing, room full
of people, one man dancing, one laughing,
another fifty or so in dead silence.
I stop laughing and join the rest.
This is a tragedy, I see. Yes,
the program says "Potato Dance,"
the famine in Ireland I think.
The man begins to pound his fist
on the potatoes, one by one
smashing them down. Now my daughter
next to me hears my suppressed laugh
I am trying hard not to let loose,
the giddy spell bottled in me
like a genie. She wheezes one good,
her glee coming out of her nose,
and we break up. A flood
overcomes us. We are weeping
for the man, letting him feed
on tears of joy when nothing's left.
The stony people, though, make us stop,
harrumphing and glaring in our direction.
Our tears dry in the fire of our shame.
Then the man bows and leaves the floor,
potato flakes in hand, mad grin on his face.

Rummaging in New Hampshire

We stop off in one of those waysides,
a converted barn—or was it
a church or town hall?—now
an antique shop in deep pine

and you love the view of the little falls
nearly undermining the hundred-year old
foundation in one corner, and you love
the churners, hoes, oars, escritoires,

apothecary bottles emptied of hope,
dusted with fingerprints that searched
for it there, wicker baskets now
a mass grave of porcelain dolls,

the blunt rafters of giant oak that shout,
"We are holding all up" as well as
the stately tone of the tall owner who's
stalked these musty aisles for fifty years.

But he reminds me of Anthony Perkins
in *Psycho* and I can't help feeling
the slant in the floor and the splintery sides
of the box holding a bunch of old diaries,

a hundred dollars for the lot. Are we not
falling down too, slowly but steadily,
our deepest hopes and dreams drifting off
for taking up by other voices and hands?

You buy an old cracked sleigh bell
in whose ring I will hear
the desolation of ages as a distant
horse chaffs away at its frozen bit.

Canyon Call

To leave the twenty-first century,
wander off the road into the canyon.
The silence is intimate like a lover
who has travelled a long distance
and now wants you all at once.

When you pause, you hear how loud
your creaking pack has been,
a rattle of coin in a quiet church.
Where a juniper cork screws into the sky,
a white gray bird with a brown back
tilts his head sidewise and flies off.

You have never been so at home
and this alone. You ask the universe,
"why have you kept my true life a secret
from me?" but you know there is no I
in this place where oceans have come and gone.

You envy clouds, wanting to rise and float,
to defy the fate that made you human.
Life on earth began in such rhythms, yes?
You think of your brother, lost along the way.
The path down is much easier than up.

Looking back, you see only your footprints
in pinkish dust that go the one way
like the river far below. Soon the sun
will kneel to darkness. Light dwindles,
and you cannot stay for long. Each step

down drops you further back in time
and cannot be retraced though sure to be
erased. You could turn into a stone,
so alone, so at home, and no one
would ever find you here, no

more than fish its fossil or shore
now cliff, each grain of sand unique
and each alike, one of many
and each one one. Is this how things stand?
An eagle's cry warns: stay on the trail.

At path's end, the river reveals its craft.
Obsidian slabs rise, cathedrals
two billion years old. When night comes,
the stars sing praise. A pink scorpion
crawls in your boot and leaves at dawn.
How lucky one is to be alive.

Walking back up, you feel left behind.
You laugh and weep, and want to tell
the world what you cannot understand,
alone at home before a desert-like page.
The canyon has claimed you, one of its own.

Mimicry

"More like the sitter than the sitter herself,"
Raphael declared of a Lippi Madonna.
The living may seek their own perfection
but never find, the painter implied,
the way a mother cannot hold a child
close enough to keep it from all harm
though that be the woman's deepest desire.
The sun would never glare in her child's eye,
for she? She would never turn away.

But Maria, Madonna's model, is hungry
and imagining pears, with none like
herself seeing herself in any way
than what she is, at least in her own eyes.
Where else would art find its light
to launch itself above our shade
than in a beauty bound to be nevermore,
with nothing else like it when it lived?

Lines etch themselves beneath our eyes.
Art though in lines finds no such doom
once freed from the tomb of the artist's hands.
It photoshops a shadow in the blank march
of days that flicker by us on our way,
a flock of birds frozen in the sky,
a sun blinding us by other means.

Sometimes we see the fatty hand of art
loom over the hand, or a portrait
not with the gait of any man that lived,
a limp counterfeit of humanity,
as Hamlet says. Sometimes we awake

to find we've been actors in our own skin.
That's when death or love throws out art,

and we find ourselves sitting in a park
on a cold slab crying hot tears,
a sad clown, our mascara dripping,
or frozen like a stone, freed by death
from having to act another's part.
Will we care then if nobody comes by
to offer a word, remark on how we look,
place a flower just so turned to the light?
It could be a common one, not even bought,
a violet plucked from a garden where a crow
seemed to mock our hand for its secret theft.

Painting the Light

I River of Light

In Caravaggio's second *Conversion,*
light falls indifferently, if anything,
more on the horse than on the saint.
The animal looks down at his fallen
master, alerted but not afraid,
set free from a burden, careful
not to hoof the man whose arms
lift up as if seeking embrace.

His bit's held tight by an old servant
whose wrinkled scalp makes a dull lamp,
foil to the shimmering stream
that glows on the blinded rider's face.
Only the horse's eyes are shown open,
mute witness to what neither man sees -

how light floods the world with shadow,
not regarding who holds the reins.

II Dark Matter (On Edward Hopper's *Summer Evening* 1947)

It's that serious moment when the party's
over. A man and woman end up alone
under a porch with its garish lightbulb
like a fake sun. The night frames the scene
with a black smirk as if it knows
it cannot be lit. The woman too
has withdrawn her view from the man
turned towards her, offering words
to her she does not need or favor

even though his hand has reached
for his heart. She's not convinced—
it's his left hand, and she's heard it
before if not from him, from others
who have eyeballed her up and down.
She knows words like light don't reveal all.

III To Joseph Roulin, Postman, Facing Van Gogh

A creature of the light, you stand
still at the mercy of the sun.
Where you live inside his pattern,
flowers rise and fall unhung.
Now you're a sea, now wild fields.
The wind whispers patience
to you, dreaming as you face him,
the frenzied stillness of his gaze
turning you into a mountain or half
an hour glass or patch of night.

Your eyes steadfastly deliver
their blue like your parcels,
across centuries, having to get
through, even your watching him
but another face of your faithfulness
to your post, the silent syllables
of your burden speaking on the other side
of the page, canvas, or grave. Outside,
a northeaster wails away,
and we too watch and must obey.

The Breach (Fire Island National Wilderness)

Gulls see land's end and cry out
at the horizontal summit
where bay and ocean merge,
any patch of sand

a lesson in near infinity,
old inlet, now new inlet,
open wound in love with stars.
I wander out to where a last

tree has a few green leaves
and a dune of sand is left
to shelter gray birds and a fox
who walks about my tent at night,

the clover leaf of his steps
among the bare prints of mine.
Just a few feet further east
and this little place of rest

would have been scooped away
and lost to the hurricane
that came with waves (as did we).
It's no breach but an opening

to the sky inside the sea.
I trace its cut in my hands
and hear it in the song of birds
and the toss and turn of dreams.

The Slant Light

(For Michael)

I love the slant light, the late light, how it
falls on everything, on a woman's face
passing by, on her dog pissing in the dune,
on one and then another seagull
over the steel gray wave whose curl
flashes white, on houses, cutting one
in half, on a rise in the sand next to
a trashcan, lighting all from below
as if it were blessing what it touches.

I tell my son how I love it, and he says,
"yes, it's nice," as he looks at his phone,
the cars speeding by like the day itself.
I ask him how many times have I
told him I so love the orange light.
He laughs. "A lot. You say it everyday."
And I say one day you'll say to your son
how your dad loved the slant light, and you'll
love him standing in it all the more.

Inside the Teaching Machine

I look down my roster at names
from all over the globe and I can't
imagine who these people are
and how they've come to me.

What can I say to them
from the fish-bowl of my world?
I stand a talking machine before them,
and I don't understand

why they don't understand.
I'm as afraid of my own ignorance
as my students are of theirs, too shy
or proud to admit or raise a hand.

We know little of each other
and a little more of ourselves.
The biggest facts show how small
we are and yet they join us here

all together in the one room
where we laugh and fret
under the dull music of some trees
and the speckled light on our desks.

I repeat myself so often
questions lose sight of the quest.
My students look at me for guidance
but their mind has to find itself

as more than a mirror of others
that mistakes a shadow for a mensch.
I teach them to read themselves,
and they must lead me to listen.

At times more than a screen lights up
the dark room where we think.
Our talk stumbles on the unknown
there where we'd slumped in our seats.

Why do we give one man such power?
Does entropy impact thought?
What have the four hundred thousand years
our race has lived on earth taught?

A silence drains me to empty
after the final test. It warns
I often failed to know the person
behind the student, or held to account

the one I answer to in my name.

IV Senescence

Works in Progress

I

In my dream I am a child again
asking me where he has gone
in the maze of possibilities that
once greeted us each morning.
I check my pockets for an answer,
perhaps a photograph in my wallet
offering a clue, but he chuckles
when I show him. "That's a picture
you have of what we looked like then,
but I am much more than a look."

He gestures me to follow along,
across the road, through a brief
tangle of trees, a field of weeds,
and then a string of new stores
which he points out were not there
in his heyday though here now
in this dream I've given him.
He leads me by the hand.
I buy myself some candy as a child.

Behind the stores a few trees
still hold on. "We never went
to the creek that ran through these woods.
I wanted to go dance. Now
it's too late. The water's gone under
the way my life's beneath yours."

Then he vanishes. I turn round to see
a set of tracks in snow that cut
a straight path except where
it breaks off to the woods.
I look there. There's a bird
in a tree, its head turned aslant.
It ponders me and flies off.

II

When I wake or think I have,
I peer down the stretch of my body
and up to the sky as if I were
a divining rod or a flower,
a channel for currents and flows,
and I know the child is my source
that can only be fleet, never seen,
like a root one must not dig up
but trusted in and kept sweet.

A loud knock jolts me as I
conjure remnants of the dream.
I call out, "what's going on up there?"
My son and friends have crashed something
in the attic where I live in the now,
his father, he who has to say
the party's over to a child
at the top of the stairs.
He looks down and runs off.

Does my dream translate into advice,
as if in secret a spirit has revealed?
Should I give this child the last word?
As if there's anyone who keeps one last,
or there can be any one of them that lasts.
The child in me wants to run off
and join my son in the wild fray,
who we are and were in tension
in our lives back and forth,
old and young interlocked.
But I have to say "no" now,
and not for a last time I am sure.
I have to act a role, a father's,
that does not sit well with him or me.
No one part is the only part
at any one time we play.
Havoc breeds paradoxes,
but even waves come to rest.

A self across time alters in dialogue
with others who want us to act our age,
but to do so requires a crossroads mind
that sees the path behind as settled
though open at both ends where one stands
as if in a meadow not seen before.

What else can a child teach me at my age,
the one I dream and the one who is his own?

The Portent

Sixty-odd years I had to log
to get this one glimpse of geese.
After a storm, heading east
between buildings over the bay,
they flashed by in heavy fog
that rose up to pale the day.

Had a shroud dropped from the sky
to hide the departure of clouds?
One can fathom reasons why,
but the honks of the flock were loud
as if warning me to see.

Since then, my mind's out to sea,
pondering my life's dark book,
and why it took so long to look.

The Grandfathers

They watch the baby dead asleep
and look up to swap their tears
as much of wonder as of joy.

To begin without knowing of an end,
to end with what one knows of the start,
who is to say who is better off?

The two men see that in each other's eyes,
how their chance in life has poured
into a river closest to the ocean

while the baby still swims oblivious
of all else besides the sea,
its mother, where the shore began.

Red Cup, Yellow Leaves

The leaves are on fire again.
Our grandson leads me by the hand
and points to the sky—"there, there."

I need no prompt to think of you.
Any star is enough. Or houses
along the shore in fog.
The lip of a cup tinged red.

And yesterday, that lost song.
I've learned to say we've danced
puts off the day we say we do.

Words can't nuzzle a page
the way your imprint lingers,
alone along this black trail,

this dance of one before
a forest of your absence.

Assistive Living

They share the camaraderie of death,
the lonely bruise that cannot heal,
a fishbowl near the light, potted
plants, the stitch that makes them friends,
common meals, and laughter that grants
the sleep keeping them from despair.
This is their final reward, their wisdom,
not wanted by those too busy or afraid
to break bread at their table and listen.

Epilogue (Transport)

Once aloft, one feels like a bird,
freed from the world, uprooted, vagrant,
a cloud, but more like a plane, enabled
by the ground, maker of the fuel.

The reeling freedom flying reveals
hides its indebted source and all
that connects to hold one in place,
family, friends, body, and home,

to which one must return.

About the Author

Anthony DiMatteo's poems, essays and reviews have been spotted roaming the pages of *The Cortland Review, College Literature, Renaissance Quarterly, Smartish Pace, Tar River Poetry,* and *Verse Daily*. His recent book *In Defense of Puppets* has been hailed as, "a rare collection, establishing a stunningly new poetic and challenging the traditions that DiMatteo (as Renaissance scholar) claims give the poet 'the last word' *(Cider Press Review)*. He is also the author of *Beautiful Problems: Poems* as well as a chapbook *Greetings from Elysium*. A former group home supervisor for a decade, he now defends the mysteries of writing, literature, and art at the New York Institute of Technology where he is a full professor of English. He happily lives with his wife, the designer and classical pianist Kathleen O'Sullivan, their sixteen-year old son Michael, a dog, and a lion-headed rabbit.

www.ingramcontent.com/pod-product-compliance
Lightning Source LLC
Chambersburg PA
CBHW021026090426
42738CB00007B/918